Original title:

Shimmering Shores of the Tropics

Copyright © 2025 Creative Arts Management OÜ
All rights reserved.

Author: Henry Beaumont
ISBN HARDBACK: 978-1-80581-644-7
ISBN PAPERBACK: 978-1-80581-171-8
ISBN EBOOK: 978-1-80581-644-7

Mellow Breezes and Ocean Blues

The palm trees dance in the breeze,
As I try to catch a buzzing bee.
Sipping coconut with a silly grin,
I'll never learn how to swim!

Seagulls squawk, they think they're cool,
But I just tripped over my own pool.
The waves laugh as they roll and sway,
It's a good day to misbehave!

Serenades Under Coconut Canopies

Under palms, we gather with snacks,
Bungee-jumping crabs plan their attacks.
The sun hides behind a funny cloud,
While we giggle, oh so loud!

Tropical drinks with tiny umbrellas,
Competitions between our silly fella.
A friendly iguana joins the fun,
Who knew napping by the beach could stun?

An Invitation to Tranquil Shores

Come join the party by the bay,
Where flip-flops stray, and seagulls play.
We'll build a castle with no crown,
And let our laughter drown the frown!

The crabs all want to be our friends,
They dance and jive as the day ends.
A coconut rolls, it takes a dive,
In this chaotic fun, we thrive!

Sunbeams Weaving Through Palm Fronds

Sunbeams peek through leaves in a tease,
As I wave to a crab, if you please.
Mismatched sandals on my feet so snug,
A wave crashes, giving me a hug!

Swinging hammocks that whirl around,
While chubby seagulls drop to the ground.
They steal our chips without a care,
Who knew their audacity was so rare?

Echoes of a Gentle Surf

The ocean's tickle on my toes,
It whispers secrets from the rose.
Seagulls squawk and dive for fish,
While crabs perform their wiggly wish.

The tide pulls back with quite a flair,
I chase my hat, it flies in air!
A jellyfish ghost dances by,
I laugh and run—oh me, oh my!

Twilight Hues on Coastal Skies

The sun dips low, a grand display,
In pinks and golds, it steals the day.
A tourist trips, his drink in hand,
He splashes colors on the sand.

Flip-flops flip, and laughter roars,
As kids build castles near the shores.
A sand crab nabs a snack and scurries,
They're quick, those crabs, no time for worries!

The Lure of Sunset's Embrace

With sunset hues that fade to night,
We gather round, all in delight.
A picnic spreads with snacks galore,
I find a crab that wants to score!

The fire pit's gone quite amiss,
Marshmallows sticking, it's hit or miss.
The moon now lights our silly dance,
But watch your step; you might just prance!

Pearlescent Seashell Chronicles

A seashell finds its way to me,
It tells of fish and jelly glee.
I hold it to my ear and grin,
It sounds like laughter from within.

The tide pulls back, the shells all huddle,
I trip and fumble through the muddle.
A conch shell laughs, it's quite the sprite,
"Hey, leave some snacks for us tonight!"

Palm Fronds and Ocean Whispers

Beneath the palms, the coconuts roll,
Somewhere a crab is losing its soul.
A flamingo dances, trying to twerk,
While tourists giggle, enjoying the perk.

Waves crash and laugh, they're quite the prank,
They splash the sunbathers, leaving them dank.
Seagulls squawk jokes, they steal all the fries,
A pirate's treasure? It's just fried pies.

The Beauty of Sunlit Shores

The sun is a giant lime in the sky,
With sunscreen on noses, they all look awry.
Beach balls float high like dreams on a string,
While sandcastles crumble—no royal bling.

Sand in your shorts is a rude little guest,
It tickles and pokes, never lets you rest.
The waves sing a tune, like a wacky old bard,
Praise be to the lifeguard; he works hard!

An Odyssey of Saltwater Dreams

Flip-flops flop loud on the boardwalk's pace,
The jellyfish jive in a gooey embrace.
Lifeguards pose like they're on a catwalk,
While sea turtles plot their next quirky talk.

Kids bury their siblings, with giggles abound,
Still, someone's lost in the sand, where'd they bound?
Seagulls plot snack heists, with plans so elaborate,
Just another day where they navigate fate.

Tidal Embrace of Tomorrow's Dawn

At dawn, the beach looks like a pastel fair,
Surfers are snoring, they're dreaming, I swear.
Crabbing with nets, a dubious side-hustle,
Turns out they catch more seaweed than muscle.

A pelican nudges, "I'm first in this queue,"
As the coffee kicks in, they all need a brew.
Coconut hats are in style, oh so bold,
But only the wise wear them—so I'm told!

The Dance of Seafoam and Sunlight

The waves prance around with glee,
As crabs take part in a seaweed spree.
Seagulls shuffle, feathers a-fluff,
While fish flip-flop in the quirky stuff.

Sunbeams bounce like a playful pup,
While beach balls leap from the ocean's cup.
Sandcastles wobble in a goofy race,
The tide's tickling feet leave a funny trace.

Lighthouses of Forgotten Dreams

A lighthouse winks at the dreamy sky,
While boats wear sunhats and seagulls fly.
Old fishermen tell tales so bold,
Of mermaids knitting socks from gold.

Waves giggle and splash, a quarrelsome lot,
As starfish dance on the warm, sunny spot.
Every so often, they stop and sway,
Mimicking tourists who forgot their way.

Moonlit Pathways Across the Bay

Moonbeams tiptoe on the water's face,
While crabs try ballet at a clumsy pace.
A dolphin whistles a silly tune,
While seaweed twirls beneath the moon.

Stars begin to chuckle in the night,
As jellyfish flash their disco light.
The breeze joins in with a joyful sigh,
Tickling everyone passing by.

Journeys Through Silken Sands

A flip-flop here and a flip-flop there,
Footprints tangled in a comical snare.
Sandy dogs roll with exaggerated flair,
While kids build forts that don't seem to care.

Kites soar high in the colorful sky,
As sandcastles crumble with a squeaky cry.
Life at the beach is a flurry of fun,
Where every sunshine day feels like a pun.

The Glittering Canvas of Dusk

In the hammock, I swing with delight,
A coconut falls, oh what a fright!
The sunset is painted in colors so bright,
But my drink spills as I sip with slight bite.

Flip-flops splashing on sand like a band,
Seagulls stealing fries, oh isn't life grand?
I dance with the crab, my new little friend,
He pinches my toe, the laughter won't end.

Drifting Dreams on Gentle Waves

A rubber duck floats, in the sea it's a prince,
While I paddle by it, my limbs move like mince.
My sunscreen's a mess, white streaks on my nose,
I'm the majestic whale covered up in rose.

Beach balls are bouncing, oh what a sight,
Flamingos dance, and it all feels so right.
Lost in the tide, my flip-flops declare,
That sandy socks are a new fashion flair!

Kaleidoscope of Sea and Serenity

The ocean's a canvas, with splashes of style,
I attempted to surf, but fell with a smile.
Seaweed now clings to my sunburned left knee,
I'm like a sea monster that's desperate to flee.

A beach chair parade, they all roll away,
The sun's getting low, Hey! Where's my toupee?
With towels as capes, we soar like the breeze,
While dodging the ice cream that's bound to tease.

The Mystique of Tropical Nocturne

As night drapes its cloak, the fireflies dance,
My mate's in a grass skirt, daring romance.
With ukuleles strumming, we sing out of tune,
While mosquitoes hold a wild, buzzing moon.

The stars seem to chuckle, they wink as they glow,
As we fail a conga, stumbling toe-to-toe.
A pineapple hat, that's my latest design,
In the land of the silly, the weird is divine.

Embracing the Vivid Horizon

An octopus wore a funny hat,
He danced with a crab, now look at that!
Seashells giggled on the sandy ground,
While fish played poker, oh, what a sound!

A parrot squawked jokes from a tree,
Sunbathers laughed, sipping their tea.
The sun chuckled as waves took a spin,
While seagulls mentored a shy dolphin's grin!

Kaleidoscope of Colors at the Water's Edge

A beach ball bounced, then rolled away,
Chasing it was a kid in dismay.
Flip-flops flew, like birds in flight,
As everyone joined the impromptu kite!

Sunsets painted red and peach,
Clowns juggled fish, what a crazy beach!
Mermaids snickered at a surfboard's flip,
While waves just laughed at the scene's weird trip!

Awakening the Spirit within the Sea

A clam complained, 'I'm stuck, help me out!'
A dolphin replied, giggling, no doubt.
Jellyfish bounced like bouncy balloons,
While turtles synchronized their silly tunes!

The shrimp formed a band, played seashell's song,
And crabs did the cha-cha, oh so wrong!
A whale told a tale, nearly made us cry,
But ended with a joke, oh my, oh my!

Horizon's Whisper Beneath Tropical Suns

A sunburned tourist searched for shade,
While lizards lounged, perfectly laid.
Surfboards stacked like a game of Jenga,
As seagulls plotted a snack on the agenda!

Sandy toes wiggled with glee,
Making friends with ants, what a sight to see!
An iguana wore sunglasses with flair,
As laughter echoed in the salty air!

Secrets Beneath the Azure Skies

A crab in a tuxedo finds such delight,
He dances on rocks, genius in his sight.
Fish gossip and giggle, they share their tales,
While seaweed sways, wearing its green veils.

A parrot on a palm preens with such flair,
He thinks he's a model, none would dare compare.
The shells hold secrets of parties gone wild,
Where starfish once waltzed, looking quite styled.

Reflections on Warm Waters

A dolphin wears shades, looking so cool,
He parks his sleek self by an island school.
Turtle races happen, all in slow motion,
They bet on seaweed, causing quite a commotion.

The waves seem to laugh as they crash on the reef,
While seagulls are stealing a beach snack—how brief!
Sandcastles stand proudly, though slightly askew,
As children then giggle, their fort now a zoo.

The Enchantment of Distant Horizons

A coconut spins, on a quest for the shore,
It's worried its milk might spill out once more.
The sunset feels quirky, wearing a grin,
As waves wear pajamas, ready for swim.

The gulls play charades, don't follow the rules,
They squawk about fish like a bunch of old fools.
Sea foam giggles, tickling toes with a splash,
While flip-flops unite for a casual bash.

Tropical Reverie in Sunlit Shades

A toucan's big beak holds secrets and snacks,
While iguanas chill with relaxed, sunny backs.
The sunbathers swim like spaghetti in line,
Crabs throw a party, saying, "We're fine!"

The beach ball inflates, is that laughter nearby?
Or maybe it's kids dreaming up ways to fly.
The rhythm of waves keeps toes in a jig,
As pineapples wear hats—a fancy old gig.

The Lure of the Aquamarine Abyss

Waves roll in, what a sight!
A crab dances in sheer delight.
With sunglasses on, it takes a stroll,
While seagulls plot to steal its roll.

Flipping flops on sandy plots,
Both humans and crabs have silly thoughts.
Fish in shades whisper with glee,
Plan a party beneath the sea!

A dolphin tries to wear a hat,
But it lands on a big old cat.
The beach ball flies into the sky,
"Catch it!" the pelican does cry.

As the sun sets with a wink,
Mermaids join us for a drink.
With laughter ringing through the night,
We dance till dawn, what pure delight!

Echoes of Paradise Underneath the Stars

Underneath the twinkling lights,
A parrot shouts, "What are those sights?"
While turtles share their best jokes,
As fishes giggle with little pokes.

A hammock sways, it's not quite right,
As a raccoon joins the moonlit fight.
Flip-flops flying, what a show,
When the crabs join in on the throw!

Underneath a coconut tree,
A catfish sings in harmony.
The stars are jealous of our fun,
Their twinkles fade as we run.

The night rolls on, no cares at all,
Until we hear a loud splish-splash call.
In paradise under skies so bright,
Even the tides laugh through the night!

Glistening Trails of Sunset's Bounty

Gold and pink paint the sky,
As fish wave their fins, oh my!
A dolphin tries to catch a wave,
With a belly flop, it has no save.

Tiki torches sway, they're quite the sight,
As crickets play their tunes of night.
A coconut falls with a thud,
It's a game for every neighborhood dud.

Seashells gather for a gossip spree,
Discussing the latest beach entry.
Just then a kid yells, "Oh no!"
As ice cream meets the sand below.

The sunset whispers all its tales,
While jellyfish start winding trails.
With laughter echoing everywhere,
This paradise gives all its flair!

Mirage of Dreams on Endless Beaches

On an endless stretch, it's all a tease,
As a seagull barked, "What's your cheese?"
Sand between toes, a twisty fate,
The waves are late, oh what a date!

A bottle rolls, what could it say?
"Help! My cap's gone astray!"
A crab steps in, types with a claw,
"Don't bother, it's just a punny law!"

At the edge, a flamingo prances,
While starfish do the tango dances.
The fun never seems to cease,
As sea cucumbers join the peace!

With a cu i journey into the seas,
The laughter grows, so full of tease.
At twilight's fall, we just can't part,
As mirages mirror every heart!

Melodies of Surf and Melody

The waves dance like they're on a date,
While crabs plot a plan, oh isn't it great?
A seagull prances, wearing shades so chic,
Screaming out tunes like a rockstar freak.

Sharks are in choir, singing off-key,
With fish doing backflips, what a sight to see!
A dolphin plays guitar, strumming so fast,
While the octopus drums, bringing a blast!

The sun winks down, a spotlight so bold,
As sandcastles giggle, their stories unfold.
A hermit crab's solo, a true showstopper,
No one can resist that little shell hopper.

At sunset, all creatures join in for a call,
Making their music, it's a beachy ball!
With laughter and bubbles, gleeful and bright,
The melodies echo, from morning to night.

The Secret Language of the Tide

Whispers of waves, a chatty delight,
Shells gossip secrets, under moonlight.
Fish trade old stories, with tales so tall,
While starfish debate who's the best at the ball.

Crabs have a dance-off, all snippy and fast,
With sandpipers judging, they're having a blast.
A turtle in shades, moves slow with the beat,
As conch shells cheer, this party's a treat!

The tide rolls in, like a curious friend,
With secrets and stories, around every bend.
But when it retreats, oh what a mess,
A seaweed fashion show, truly a jest!

As day turns to night, the stars start to glow,
Making waves' laughter, a nighttime show.
The moon takes a bow, all creatures unite,
In the secret language, of joy and delight!

Vibrant Horizons and Ocean Whispers

The sun wears shades, it's quite a sight,
With flip-flops dancing from morning to night.
Crabs in the sand hold a tiny parade,
While seagulls squawk jokes that never quite fade.

A coconut drinks a piña colada,
While fish in the sea sing a fun bravada.
Surfboards are rolling, some take a dive,
Just watch for the turtle, he's in for a jive.

Kids build castles that lean to the right,
A sandcastle king preparing for flight.
The tide comes in, and they scurry in fear,
But wave-dodging laughter is all that we hear.

At dusk when the sky paints a wacky hue,
Beach umbrellas sway and a crab joins the crew.
With laughter and splashes, we all share a grin,
Life on this shore is a joyful din.

Nature's Mosaic by the Water

The sun spills salsa on glistening sand,
While jellyfish juggle, just look at them strand!
Palm trees are swaying, they tickle the breeze,
And turtles roll by with the greatest of ease.

Sunglasses squint at a curious crab,
Who steals all the snacks with a crafty grab.
The fish throw a party, they splash and they tease,
While dolphins play pictionary with ease.

A piña colada delivers a grin,
While tourists are breaking their dance moves akin.
The pelicans waddle with utmost precision,
In a world where each wave holds a new mission.

As sunset approaches, flamingos gossip,
While everyone else tries to find a good spot.
The laughter, the splashing, this vibrant affair,
In nature's collage, fun hangs in the air.

Peaceful Shores and Timid Waves

The beach is a stage, and here comes the tide,
With waves that whisper, "Come join in the ride!"
Seashells are nestled like nuggets of gold,
While a crab sidesteps, all bashful and bold.

Sunburnt tourists play chase with the sun,
While a seagull makes off with a hot dog run.
The sand is a blanket where laughter can spread,
And sandcastles tumble with each wave that's fed.

A wise old turtle shares tales from the sea,
Of mermaids and treasures, so wild and so free.
Kids giggle and splatter with every small splash,
While the sunset makes magic in colors that clash.

With picnic leftovers flying through the air,
And a sneaky raccoon that's bold and quite rare.
The beach holds a treasure of smiles and delight,
Where fun in the chaos makes everything right.

Land of Endless Sunsets

In a land where sunsets paint cheeky skies,
The horizon stumbles, but no one denies.
Fish dance in circles, with no shoes to wear,
While crabs hold their meetings, all bumbling with flair.

The coconut smiles, a tropical king,
As flip-flops are lost while folks start to sing.
Sun hats get tossed in a playful embrace,
While sunscreen battles the sun's warm, bright face.

A picnic basket filled with laughter and fun,
Tossed to the wind, "Catch it if you run!"
And as night settles in with a carnival glow,
The stars twinkle jokes that only we know.

So gather your friends for this wild, crazy ride,
With waves as our witnesses and laughter our guide.
In this land of great sunsets, the mirth's never done,
Where each day brings memories, all woven in sun.

Twilight's Touch on Tropical Dreams

The sun dips low, a giant eye,
A coconut falls with a wobbly sigh.
Palm trees sway in a clumsy dance,
While crabs roll by in a beachside prance.

Flip-flops slap on the sandy floor,
Seagulls squawk with a cheeky roar.
A hermit crab dons a bottle's cap,
Thinking it's stylish—it takes a nap.

The waves greet me with a splash and a laugh,
As I trip over my own goofy path.
Sandcastles crumble without much fuss,
Just like my hair, an unruly rust!

Under stars that twinkle like bouncing lights,
I dance with shadows, no worries, no fights.
The ocean hums its quirky tune,
As laughter mingles with the bright, ballooned moon.

A Dance of Nature's Palette

Colors clash like a playful fight,
In landscapes brushed with pure delight.
Sunsets exploding in vibrant cheer,
While turtles waltz; oh, look at them steer!

A rainbow parrot gives a wink and a squawk,
As I stumble over the colorful block.
The mango trees are messy and bold,
Dropping fruit like treasures to behold.

Fish in the tide perform a quick jig,
While I attempt to limbo, feeling quite big.
Palm leaves whisper jokes to the breeze,
Swaying in laughter, oh such a tease!

With each fluffy cloud, my imagination soars,
I join in the dance on the sandy floors.
The night is a canvas where dreams take flight,
As we giggle and twirl under stars shining bright.

Seashells and Solitary Strolls

A single shell holds a secret or two,
It once had a home for a crab or a crew.
I pick it up and pretend it can chat,
It tells me of fish and a hat-wearing cat!

Each step in the sand feels like a slip,
With wedged toes making a hilarious trip.
Seagulls laugh overhead in a feathered show,
As I practice my runway walk—oh no, whoa!

The tide rolls in with a giggly tease,
As waves tickle toes like mischievous bees.
I wave to the jellyfish, they wave back in style,
Their jiggly dance makes me grin all the while.

Collecting memories like starfish on shore,
Each one's a treasure I simply adore.
As the sun fades slowly beyond the wide sea,
I laugh at my footprints, what a sight to see!

Memories Carried by Ocean Currents

The ocean whispers tales, full of fun,
Where dolphins race and catch the sun.
I sit on the shore, a snack in my pack,
Fighting off seagulls who plot a bold snack!

Waves crash in giggles, flipping my hat,
The tide bubbles up like a playful cat.
I watch the horizon chase the bright sky,
While deciding which fruit is my next favorite pie!

A ship sails by with its sails full of pride,
But the captain waves back with a wobbly slide.
Seaspray tickles my laughter with glee,
As I grab handfuls of sand - oh, so carefree!

With each rolling wave, I feel the bliss,
Memories float by, not a moment I miss.
The day bows out with a firework glow,
As I dance with the sea, where good vibes flow.

The Secret Language of Gentle Waves

The waves chat wildly, they splash and they tease,
Whispering secrets to legs feeling weak.
A crab with sharp claws makes a bold stance,
While fish giggle softly at the beach's dance.

Seagulls debate with a squawk and a caw,
Judging the beachgoers, what a sight to draw.
A flip-flop flies as a child takes a leap,
And sandy umbrellas stand tall in their sleep.

Sunbathers laugh in a dance of great flair,
While sunscreen's aroma is filling the air.
The sand builds castles, a kingdom from dreams,
Where jellyfish kings plot aquatic regimes.

So come, hear the whispers, the laughs of the tide,
In this silly kingdom where creatures abide.
Waves crash with humor, oh what a display,
Join the chorus of fun at the end of the day.

Paradise Paints its Palettes at Dawn

The sun winks playfully, painting the skies,
As roosters sing loudly, much to our surprise.
Pineapples giggle in their fruity parade,
While coconuts roll like a laugh in the shade.

A hammock swings softly, it beckons with grace,
While flip-flops race each other, a footwear race.
The coffee is laughing, with a frothy big smile,
As dolphins do somersaults, oh, what a while!

Juicy mangoes whisper with a fruity cheer,
While palm trees sway, nearly spilling their beer!
And sunburned tourists swap tales of their fights,
As crabs plan their heist in the warm morning lights.

So raise a coconuts drink with a chuckle or two,
In this bright paradise, there's much fun to do.
The dawn paints the morning in colorful schemes,
As laughter unfolds in this land of our dreams.

A Serenade of Light on Turquoise Waters

The sun dances lightly, with glimmers of fun,
While mermaids gossip, all golden and spun.
The water is laughing, it shimmers with glee,
As turtles race by on their slow-motion spree.

A pelican drops in to try a new dive,
While fishes form bands, making tunes to arrive.
Beach balls bounce cheerfully in playful delight,
When beachgoers tumble, what a comical sight!

A toddler's splash echoes, a joyful embrace,
While seagulls engage in an aerial chase.
The tide plays the trumpet, each wave a sweet sound,
As laughter erupts from the shores all around.

So listen to the waters, and join in the fun,
This serenade of light has only begun.
Splash into the chuckles, let merriment play,
On these turquoise waters, let joy light the way.

Celestial Dreams on Soft Sand

Stars twinkle down like confetti of dreams,
As sandcastles giggle in moonlight's soft beams.
A beach ball is floating, quite lost in the night,
While crickets chirp disco with sheer delight.

The moon's a cool DJ, spinning tunes on the shore,
As waves come in rhythm, calling out for more.
Starfish hold parties, with fish on the guest list,
Who knew the beach had an evening twist?

Mermaids in whistles, they beckon to dance,
While surfers show off with a wave-riding prance.
Glow worms are lighting up the sandy sweet stage,
Where laughter and joyousness flow, age to age.

So dream on the soft sand, let silliness soar,
Each pulse of the ocean unlocks a new door.
In celestial moments, watch life's playful stand,
And giggle 'til dawn on this magical sand.

Echoes of Serenity in the Gentle Surf

A crab in a tux, moves with great flair,
He thinks he's the king, of this sandy lair.
Sun hats on turtles, they laugh and they play,
While the waves giggle softly and sway all day.

Seagulls are gossiping, who wears the best hat?
The octopus blends in, just like a sly cat.
They trade ocean stories, all silly and grand,
As fish flash their fins, in a synchronized band.

The starfish are judges, on the beach there's a game,
Who tells the best joke? It's never the same.
The winner gets seaweed, all sticky but sweet,
And a chance to decide the next seafood treat.

So come join the laughter, dance on the sand,
With crabs and sea gulls, it's a wild band.
In the gentle surf's echo, life's a fun spree,
With a tickle from waves, come splash along with me!

Lullabies of the Ocean's Embrace

The waves sing to shells, like babies in cribs,
While dolphins perform, with remarkable jibs.
A seaweed plush toy, for a tired old fish,
Their dreams drift away, like a wispy wish.

Mermaids are strumming, on clam-shell guitars,
Singing out tales 'neath the twinkling stars.
With bubbles as chorus, they splash and they cheer,
While fish form a line, for a song that they hear.

The crabs throw a party, with snacks made of sand,
A dance-off erupts, it's a jiggly band.
Jellyfish glow bright, in the limelight of night,
While the ocean hums soft, it feels just right.

By morning's soft blush, they all wave goodbye,
Tentacles winding, under the blue sky.
Every shell has a story, full of whimsy and glee,
In the lulled embrace, come sway along with me!

Coastal Secrets in a World of Gold

The sand is so warm, it sparkles with cheer,
While seagulls make plans, for their pie in the pier.
A crab's on a mission, with a bucket of fries,
He offers them round, with the best of disguise.

The tide pools are treasure, filled with odd sights,
Where starfish compete, in the silliest fights.
They laugh and they wobble, on rocks that are slick,
With moody old urchins, who just like to trick.

A pelican's hat, a beak that's so bright,
He wears shades of rainbow, just to look right.
He swoops down to snag, a snack from the shore,
While octopuses cheer, laughing more and more.

With secrets of gold in the breeze's soft flow,
The laughter erupts where the goofy things go.
So join in the fun, let the day drift away,
Where the coast holds its secrets, and giggles don't stay!

The Enchantment of Daylight's Dance

The sun dips and sways, like a dancer with flair,
While crabs grab the tide, and join in midair.
The fish tell their tales, with winks and with flips,
It's a splash-tastic show, with bubbly quips.

Seagulls are buzzing, with gossip to share,
While sea urchins grumble, caught in a snare.
A clam with a grin, sings out to the crowd,
Fridays are fun days, he's feeling so proud.

And here come the mermaids, with choreographed lines,
Waving their tails like fancy designs.
They glide through the sea, with a twirl and a spin,
As the tide starts to hum, inviting us in.

With every bright ray, the day twinkling sings,
The ocean ignites, like a party with wings.
So gather your mates, let the fun take its stance,
In the magic of sunlight, come join in the dance!

Tales from Vibrant Coral Gardens

Underwater fish in tiny cars,
Zooming past our picnic jars.
A crab wearing shades shimmies by,
With a dance that makes the jellyfish cry.

The octopus serves drinks on a tray,
But spills it all in a colorful way.
Laughing dolphins do a flip,
While we try not to spill our chips.

The Allure of Sun-Drenched Paradise

A sunburned seagull steals my fries,
With a wink it charms the blue skies.
Beachgoers chase a runaway hat,
As a surfer yells, 'Dude! Look at that!'

Sandy toes and sunscreen goop,
We gather round for the beachside loop.
With laughter echoing in the breeze,
Everyone joins in with utmost glee.

Flavors of Tropical Euphoria

Coconut drinks and silly straws,
Sipping slowly—oops! What's that? A cause!
A pineapple wearing sunglasses,
Raises a toast - who needs big mamas?

Mango sticky rice on a raft,
Lost at sea, now that's a laugh!
Banana boats zooming fast,
Hope the humor forever lasts.

Tides Caressing Hidden Coves

Waves crashing on a sandy stage,
The hermit crabs all start to engage.
With little paws, they clap and cheer,
And shout, 'Dance, human! Bring the beer!'

In hidden nooks, the treasures lie,
A flip-flop found, 'Oh my!' they cry.
Nature's game of hide and seek,
In this paradise, life's never bleak.

Chasing the Glow of Coastal Mornings

With coffee cups perched high on a dock,
A seagull swoops down—did it just steal my sock?
Waves giggle and splash as the sun gets in line,
Where laughter dances bright, and the beach feels divine.

The sand's hot enough to fry an egg, oh dear,
Flip-flops skip like children, fueled by good cheer.
Crabs scuttle along, doing their silly parade,
While sunbathers fearlessly claim their sun-made charade.

Coconuts tumble as folks try to catch,
That one flying gal whose beach style's unmatched.
Bikini tops snagged by a swift ocean breeze,
Leave us all laughing, like it's one big tease.

Every wave whispers secrets of joy in the breeze,
As I chase angry gulls, begging them for peace.
In this vibrant chaos, I find my sweet spot,
Life's a funny dance, and I've really got a lot!

A Symphony in Caribbean Colors

Colors are blaring like a stray noisy band,
With the tangerine sun playing tambourine on sand.
Pineapples bobbing like loud hula-hoops,
My sunburned neighbors make quite the funny swoops.

Dancers whirl by, all in mismatched flip-flops,
While tourist kids giggle, selling lemonade pops.
Queen conch in the shade muttering tales of delight,
While I try these moves that look good in my mind but not quite right.

A framework of palm trees sways like a crowd,
While I've lost my sunglasses under a coconut cloud.
The locals chuckle and trade their sly glances,
For I have misstepped right into a crab's dances.

Yet amidst all the colors, laughter is key,
This playful mayhem feels as good as can be.
As my drink tips over, spilling all over my toes,
I lift up my spirits, in this glorious dose!

Paradise Found in Twilight's Embrace

As the sun melts down like a giant scoop of ice,
The beach turns to magic—Oh, what a slice!
A crab in a bowtie dances on the sand,
While I'm juggling coconuts, not quite as planned.

Glowsticks twinkle, like soft-spoken dreams,
As the fireflies plot out their own little schemes.
Someone's karaoke echoes, a cat gone awry,
But we all clap along, with no thought of goodbye.

People roasting marshmallows too close to the flame,
Their hair now resembling a funny old game.
As chips dip into salsa, splattering the air,
We share all our stories without any care.

In this twilight embrace, laughter's our guide,
With each silly moment, our worries subside.
As the stars peek out from behind clouds that tease,
We toast to the chaos, under palm trees' ease!

Radiant Tides and Flirting Shadows

The waves play tag with the toes of the sun,
While dolphins leap high, having a splash-tastic fun.
Flip-flop fashion shows cause quite a buzz,
With the fashion police made of curious fuzz.

Tides lurch with a chuckle as they flirt with the moon,
While tourists tan their bellies in the heat of noon.
A sandcastle army ready to wage its great scheme,
But the tide giggles back, and they're gone like a dream.

An adventurous seagull steals my lunch with finesse,
Each nibble a triumph, I just must confess.
Sunsets whisper jokes, painting all with delight,
Turns out paradise is filled with sheer silly light.

As shadows grow long, making silhouettes dance,
We laugh at each mishap, this stepped-in-dance.
No need for perfection here, just fun on repeat,
In this wacky romance, there's strength in the heat!

Where Time Dances at the Water's Edge

The sun rolled in like a beach ball,
As seagulls squawked in a brawl.
Flip-flops flew from a quick-footed chap,
Landing smack on a sunbather's lap.

Children in buckets build castles of sand,
While a crab scuttles off, quite unplanned.
Laughter echoes as waves come to tease,
With ice cream dripping in a sticky breeze.

Floaties abound in a rainbow parade,
As grumpy dad takes a sunblock upgrade.
Mom's by the grill, flipping fish with a grin,
While dad checks the score on his phone—what a win!

When dusk paints the sky in brassy hues,
Uncle Joe's now wearing his mullet hairdo.
Time dances here, where the beach chairs sway,
And every small mishap makes our day.

Restless Waves and Golden Horizons

The waves come in, a rambunctious tide,
Chasing beachgoers who try to hide.
Bikini tops fly like flags in the breeze,
While burly dudes try to look at ease.

Fried plantains sizzle on hot little grills,
While flip-flop wearers avoid all the spills.
A child yells, "Watch me, I'm going to leap!"
And lands right on grandpa, asleep in a heap.

Sunsets in orange, a colourful scene,
Where sunscreen fights tan lines like a pair of fiends.
A seagull swoops down with a sneaky little peep,
Swiping a snack, oh what fun it can keep!

As night unfurls its starlit cloak,
The campfire tales bring forth a good joke.
We laugh as the ocean waves roll in,
Celebrating each goofy little win.

Echoes of Parrots in the Breeze

Bright parrots squawk in their feathered attire,
While beachside huts sell coconut cider.
A tourist trips over a color-blind crab,
Leaving locals laughing, "Well, that's quite fab!"

Waves slide in with a playful rush,
While someone's hat flies off in a hush.
Sandcastles crumble with giggles ensued,
As a dog runs by, happy and rude.

The hammock sways with a gentle sigh,
As Chuck talks of fishing, his catch a white lie.
Flops and flops, that's the name of the game,
But who needs fish when you've got a good name?

With echoes of laughter and tropical cheer,
We celebrate quirks that only we see here.
Beneath swaying palms, life's a party so fine,
In this merry paradise, oh how we shine!

Coconuts and Canvas Skies

Coconuts drop, and people take care,
To dodge the bombs from the trees up there.
Beach balls bounce, and laughter fills air,
With every splashed sidewalk, a happy affair.

The canvas skies paint a shade so bright,
While a parrot mimics a tourist's delight.
Sandy footprints lead to tasty delights,
As Aunt Sue claims her margarita ignites.

Beach umbrellas pop up like mushrooms in spring,
With a chorus of voices that rise up to sing.
The chorus of fun, it's contagious, you see,
As everyone joins in with glee by the sea.

As twilight creeps in with a fizzy dance,
We dance 'round the fire; it's a cosmic romance.
With coconuts brimming with juice and good cheer,
We toast to the mishaps, "Here's to next year!"

Footprints on a Warming Beach

Sandy toes and sunburned noses,
Crabs are sneaking, striking poses.
With flip-flops lost, we laugh and dive,
Who needs a map? This beach's alive!

Seagulls squawk, stealing our fries,
As we chase them, oh what a surprise!
Sun hats askew, we're quite the sight,
Trying to dance, we trip with delight!

The ocean waves call, 'Come, take a dip!'
But watch out now, or you might slip!
Splash fights galore, we're children once more,
Forgotten worries washed ashore.

As sunset paints the sky in gold,
We gather shells, stories retold.
Our footprints dance, and laughter sings,
Oh, what joy this shoreline brings!

Twilight's Brush on Oceanic Blues

Twilight descends with a splash and a grin,
Fish are flopping, it's a true win!
With my beach ball slide, you can't catch me,
If you throw a towel, you'll get soaked, you'll see!

A starfish whispers secrets untold,
While I trip on mermans' glittering gold.
Tide pools giggle with crabs in their game,
Pretending they're kings, it's quite the claim!

The moon shines down, like a disco ball,
We're dancing on water, just two inches tall.
A jellyfish floats, says, "Join the spree!"
But I run away—neither graceful nor free!

The lighthouse beams with a wink and a laugh,
I take a tumble—oh, what a gaffe!
But with waves of fun, we will never mope,
Beneath twinkling stars, we drift and hope!

Murmurs of Coconut Palms

Coconuts fall with a thud and a bounce,
While I dodge and weave—what a clumsy dance!
The palm trees giggle as breezes do sway,
They gossip of tourists in bright, bold array.

Each rustling leaf has a tale of its own,
Of sun-kissed blunders, never alone.
With a mud pie kit and a bucket of dreams,
We create castles, or so it seems!

Parrots squawk fashion tips, oh so loud,
'Wear your shades and be beachy proud!'
As I slip on my shades stuck with sand,
I strike a pose—this look's in demand.

But oh, the heat! It's turning me fried,
As I dance with the locals, feeling quite wide.
We'll laugh and we'll twirl, 'til the day bids adieu,
With memories made, in this tropical view!

A Symphony of Ocean Whispers

Waves whisper softly, 'We're back for more!'
As I trip on the tide, belly flop to the shore.
Seashells sing songs of treasures so sweet,
Only to find, I'm on my backside, neat!

Cranky old dolphins can't stop their prancing,
While flounders and fish just can't stop glancing.
With a piña colada, I'm feeling quite bold,
'Here's looking at you!'—sips of sweet gold!

The currents clown around in a bubbly parade,
Ducks and turtles join in with a serenade.
A rogue wave rolls in, we're swept up in play,
Tumbling like laundry, no worries today!

With a sunset encore, the day takes a bow,
We applaud as the ocean says, "See you now!"
As stars fill the sky, we dance in the foam,
In this symphony's heart, we find our home!

Golden Sands and Turquoise Dreams

On golden beaches, crabs dance in line,
With tiny top hats and drinks that are fine.
Seagulls gossip while the sun starts to rise,
In flip-flops they strut, oh, how they disguise!

Palm trees gossip, they wiggle and sway,
Telling tales of tourists who lost their way.
A sunscreen slip turns a frown to a cheer,
As laughter erupts, it's the highlight of the year.

Where Sunlight Kisses the Sea

Waves tickle toes, what a silly old game,
While dolphins dive in with a splash and a name.
Sunburned tourists earn spots on the wall,
With flamingo floats ready for a brawl!

Tanning has nuances, it's not just a lie,
Coconut drinks stir some fun in the sky.
While beach balls are bouncing, someone trips on a snack,
And laughter erupts as they tumble back!

Coral Serenade at Dawn

In coral patches, fish wear their best suits,
Wiggling around like they're chasing their boots.
A clownfish giggles at a pretentious star,
Saying, "Look at me! I'm the best by far!"

Morning rays glisten, and shells start to sing,
While crabs hold a meeting to gossip and bling.
With sunglasses perched on a hermit crab's head,
They plot for the day, filling seashells with bread.

Lullabies of the Ocean Breeze

The breeze tells secrets; it ruffles my hair,
While flip-flops play music, they dance without care.
Sandcastles wobble, they're laughing away,
As seashells conspire to steal the parade.

Tide pools are home to the world's best chefs,
Cooking up wonders with none of the stress.
Each wave brings a giggle, a splash in the sun,
Where humor and joy meet for playtime and fun!

www.ingramcontent.com/pod-product-compliance
Lightning Source LLC
Chambersburg PA
CBHW072136070526
44585CB00016B/1703